Evolve

Dr. Robert O'Keefe Hassell

Foreword by:
Prophet Elder Durale Lamont Kenner

BK
ROYSTON
Publishing

BK Royston Publishing
P. O. Box 4321
Jeffersonville, IN 47131
502-802-5385
http://www.bkroystonpublishing.com
bkroystonpublishing@gmail.com

Cover Design: Brent Barnett
besquaredgraphicdesign@gmail.com

ISBN-10:1-946111-34-1
ISBN-13:978-1-946111-34-0

Printed in the United States of America

Dedication

A Letter to Others Just Like Me.....

Hey! First, I want you to know that there are people who love you, care, and want to see you succeed. At this point in your life, you may feel lost, forgotten or even insignificant. I want you to know you MATTER. Your life is VALUABLE. Everything you have experienced up until this point is a manner of preparation. You have seen a lot. You have lived through tough times coupled with trauma. You have carried the heaviest weights, but they have not crushed you.

If a few people had told me I would be who I am today, I would have told them they were lying. Looking at myself now, some things are even hard for me to believe. I will tell you though, absolutely

ANYTHING (and I do mean anything) is possible! There is a world that awaits you. There is someone just like you who is watching you and needs you to make it. You have nothing to lose and everything to gain! GO FOR IT!

Pursue with Promise,

Dr. Robert O'Keefe Hassell

Foreword

Someone asked me, "Prophet Kenner, what is the meaning behind your quote? "Everything that God has ever said about you – IT HAS TO HAPPEN!" (Kenner, Durale Lamont 2008) - *Quotes That Birth Life 2010*. I responded, "Oftentimes, we use the essence of our past to bring clarification to our present. When our present understands this, it will not be in this state long. Then and only then can we "Evolve" manifesting Change."

Our manifestation is not deemed by feeling; it is deemed by agreement. Therefore, prophecy is the umbilical cord to life nourished through words spoken. The totality of a man is in who he is, what he is, and who he belongs to! Through many of life's ups and downs, forward and backward experiences, I've learned God doesn't need another you - He has who He wants.

One of my greatest experiences that caused an "Evolution" within my heart, soul and mind, is when I forgave my birth father of an incident that occurred more than twenty years ago. I remember it like it was yesterday, the day was Thursday, April 29th, 2010, I considered the hazel eyes of my father and said these words to him as tears flowed from my hazel eyes. "Dad, I hated you, when I needed you, you were not there. I despised you. I was angry. Some of the issues I went through I would have never encountered had you been there."

He responded, "Son, I did to you what my father did to me!"

I am on the verge of either mending or destroying further a broken relationship with my reaction to his comment. I chose to "Evolve" into the destined person of purpose that God had created me to be even though this hurt me tremendously. This was my moment to mirror my father, having the same traits, experiences and thought patterns. I chose to develop [Evolve] from a simple mindset to a more complex mind. After all, "How can one be full of who they are unless they have been emptied of what they were!" (Kenner, Durale Lamont 2007. Quotes That Birth Life 2010). This became bigger than he and I. This could implement the beginning of a greater relationship, respect factor and advancement for healing.

I concluded with these words to my father, "Dad, had I never been afflicted, I would have never known I could be healed!" My father dropped his head in the cup of my shoulder and he then knew he was forgiven.

"Evolve," it is my belief that this life-changing, transparent and well written release will bring wholesomeness, progression, a rejuvenation of one's purpose by life's undesired lessons and its patience to be developed into an unimaginable victorious testament. No matter how life has cut you down, you can grow again. No matter what your roots have experienced, if planted correctly, you can bud again.

Dr. Robert O'Keefe Hassell, has given us, the believer and unbeliever a rebirth to faith, rebirth to believe again; a rebirth to explore the intricacies that distinguished between life and death. Through his experiences, one can view the pureness of intention that everyone has purpose, they just need someone to activate them. I admonish you the reader to receive this selfless declaration of one man's desire to [evolve] into greatness.

Prophet Elder Durale Lamont Kenner

Author, *Quotes That Birth Life*

Refreshing Springs Church of God in Christ

Kokomo, Indiana

Table of Contents

Commendation

It is with great joy that I pen this commendation on behalf of Dr. Robert O'Keefe Hassell, who is an anointed, intelligent, and articulate man that is used mightily by God. It is clearly evident that Dr. Hassell understands the concept to *Evolve*, as he shares with you the many aspects of this process.

Dr. Hassell is phenomenal in his presentation of his real life experiences, which becomes a realistic picture of our lives as we *Evolve* into our changing selves. His book helps us to realize that God has a plan for everyone and we must tap into it by discovering who we are. We must be free in our minds and hearts to *Evolve* into our best selves for our life's journey. Dr. Hassell is transparent enough in his book to help us all *Evolve* in our journey, by helping us to understand that our mistakes, hardships, disappointments, and pains in life's experiences can make us better and not remain bitter. Things of the past should become stepping stones rather than stumbling blocks. This book produces hope to everyone who's looking for change in their lives. No matter what we face in life, we are not the only ones to experience these things. There are so many others just like us.

Dr. Hassell shows us how to pay attention to ourselves by letting us know that we have to be honest with ourselves, which helps us to grow and move forward. Doing so will help us to accept the shifts that takes place to *Evolve*. The hurtful remarks from others and battling low self-esteem should make us stronger in our perception of that which we will become, if we would only embrace change and use it to make us better on a daily basis. Doing this will help us discover many things, but it will mainly wake up the champion that is within us. God is preparing us for the next great thing in our future and there is more to us that meets the eye.

This book will help you find out more about yourself than ever before. The focus of this book is to help you learn how to be free, and stay free, with the help of

God. *Evolve* is a must read, and must share book, that will bless many for centuries to come.

Having boundaries in place will keep us aligned with what matters most in our lives. Dr. Hassell shares his own experiences with us, so that we will know that a life of crocked lines can be made straight once we *Evolve* into our greatest potential. We must not let the enemy of doubt within us, do us in. We must have faith to grow. The more we grow, the more we live. The more we live, the more we learn. Life really is worth living, and by believing this, we *Evolve*!

Bishop Belita McMurry-Fite
Senior Pastor/Founder of Heaven's View Baptist
Church
Lebanon, Tennessee

Introduction

Yes, I know there are no road maps. There is no one willing to listen or understands the depth of what you feel right now. There is so much going on in your life simultaneously at one time. Every issue is weighty combined with your emotions and multiplied by your anxiety concerning the future. It is hard to keep up. You have critical decisions to make. You are searching for answers. Whether you know it or not, you are GROWING. You are SHIFTING. You are EVOLVING. The transitions may not look like what you imagined and the landscape of your life may differ from what you planned.

Remember, time has a way of growing, establishing and defining who you will become. Whether you want to or not, time is going to make you change for the good or the better. Your decisions coupled with your actions will determine the result. Where you are now is not where you will remain. You will make mistakes. You will fall at times and it will hurt, but you serve a God that forgives completely.

Remember, your failures do not define your future. Be honest with yourself. Get up quickly. Square your shoulders and try again. It only ends when you choose to stay down.

Pursue with Promise,

Dr. Robert O'Keefe Hassell

EVOLVE

Chapter 1

"EVOLVE: The Context of Change"

"Change is at the very core of evolution, and without it all creatures would look and behave the same way."

Martin Dansky, Canadian Actor

My life can clearly be defined by the principle of the theory of evolution. "The basic theory of evolution is surprisingly simple. It has three essential parts: It is possible for the DNA of an organism to occasionally change, or mutate. A mutation changes the DNA of an organism in a way that affects its offspring, either immediately or several generations down the line. The change brought about by a mutation is beneficial, harmful or neutral" (Bogin, 1999). When we think of change, we often think of making strides to be different for

1

the moment. However, life requires us to go through a series of changes that pits who we are at the moment against who we are becoming. Change, in the greatest sense, is an evolutionary matter. Evolution is your life readily adapting to the conditions of an ever-changing world. We enter the world with an identity that is uniquely ours. We are, often, under-developed and unready to meet the demands that are placed upon us. As a result, this requires us to go through places of success and failure coupled with the relentless nature to see ourselves become the embodiment of our dreams.

Looking back over the years, the O'Keefe you see today is a direct result of lending myself to life's evolutionary process. They say life is a result of your decisions and I would wholeheartedly agree. However, when you have made all the "right decisions" there are external factors that you find yourself submitting to in order to position yourself for refinement and processing in life. Yes, it felt like I had no control at times, but it was an essential measure of fluidity that created space for me to grow beyond the places I had originally planned for each phase of my life. As a budding adolescent and young adult, there were many times I felt helpless. I cried a lot behind closed doors. Often time, my prayer times with God before bed were riddled with tears. More often than not, I would fall asleep on my knees and wake up about 2:30 a.m. to crawl in the bed to rest. However, even amid all the crying (which some would chalk up to being over emotional) I believed that God would give me an answer. In life, we ask for answers to provide not only direction, but to ease our fears regarding what awaits us at the next level.

3

We seek to take the one answer and make it "the answer," which is not always the case. Answers come to give clarity to where we presently are, and provide a frame of reference to what we are going into in our life. Life creates this unique sensation of push and pull, which makes answers seem so sufficient, yet insufficient in their ability to put to rest every place of questioning within our lives. However, in my little mind I was searching for an answer. I did not realize there would be a series of subsequent answers as my life would begin to take shape and evolve. I was such a tough little guy. I was a highly advanced adolescent, a focused individual full of energy, and would become a consistent over-achieving man who would become a 'Golden Boy' in the eyes of people. Yet, despite my successes on any level, I did not honestly know who I was at all.

EVOLVE

It would take me from age 17 to age 31 to finally figure it out. I had to fast forward my thinking and put myself on a fast track to establish a future that was tied up in decisions, choices, seizing opportunities fearlessly and practicing integrity. The 17-year-old me did not have time to think about who I was not. The 31 year old me would arrive at a place I thought was a promised land, only to learn it was an "undiscovered country" that was a rebuild. It was actually the place of freedom to create and finally be who I always wanted to become.

The theory states, "If the change is harmful, then it is unlikely that the offspring will survive to reproduce, so the mutation dies out and goes nowhere. If the change is beneficial, then it is likely that the offspring will do better than other offspring and will reproduce more. Through reproduction, the beneficial mutation spreads. The process of culling bad mutations and spreading good mutations is called natural selection. As mutations occur and spread over long periods of time, they cause new species to form" (Wood, 2002). For 14 years of my life, the journey from high school to college and subsequently college through graduate school, a battle would ensue as I struggled to fight in order to become the person you experience today. I did not realize at the moment that there would be periods of self-doubt, struggles with validation, giving away pieces of myself in efforts to be wanted, being taken advantage of, yielding to influences that were distractions as well as destructive, making some really stupid choices, being stuck in situations I had no business in at all, and wasting time. All culminating with the embracing of my manhood in its truest form, the completion of my doctorate combined with real life and the awakening of who I really was. It would be the crucible of testing for me and most definitely the fight of my life. No matter what I did, no matter how many academic feats I obtained or how great of a minister I had become in the church arena, I was in a fight and I knew it.

It is an interesting paradox how you can present peace to the outside world, but actually live in war internally. The battle for change was a constant struggle filled with many days of victory, defeat and sometimes retreats. Reflection equates perception, and we use our perception to craft our identity. I was challenged to build who I would become at an early age. Some would see that as an overwhelming thing for a child to carry, let alone do. However, I knew what people saw in me was left entirely up to their perception and not what was really inside of me. God was the center of it all. Greatness was inside of me. Brilliance was my way of life. Joy was the fuel behind my development. Laughter was healing. Hope was the force that gave me a reason to live.

High school was a unique experience for me. 1999-2003, yes those 4 years seemed to fly by. I was a fresh 17 year old; of course, like most teenagers, in my mind, I thought I would be going to high school forever. You enter in as a freshman knowing that senior year is coming. Nevertheless, it is something that hits you in the face quick once you reach that place. High school was no struggle. It was easy to climb the social ranks with minimal effort. I just simply had to find my niche and literally be able to survive amid the hormones and attitudes. It was at this level that I discovered my charm, goofiness, and articulate nature. Amid my quirkiness, there were tools that would definitely work in my favor. How that would translate into a new environment, I really had no idea. However, I was sure I had a viable combination of something that could be great and definitely memorable in people's minds. Up pops May, and I am walking across the stage to get this high school diploma. Graduation came with so many feelings. I was a high school honor graduate with full-ride scholarship offers to multiple universities. I was scared and I felt unready to face my future. I had to leave my friends. All I left high school with was a head full of knowledge, college credit, a 10-year plan, and a diploma that said I had met requirements as mandated by the state. I was literally leaving people who I had grown up with all of my life and move forward into unknown territory at a university where I would build new relationships. Unlike many of my peers, I decided to "chuck the deuces" and head 3 hours west to Lane College. I figured that getting away from the familiar, but not too far away, would provide the opportunity for me to grow into the person I was destined to become, but did not recognize at the time.

The reality about leaving home and going to a place where you know absolutely no one is a great teacher. You soon discover what you "are" and what you "are not." Your perspective on life and your subsequent surroundings change. Your boundaries re-adjust. You find yourself asking questions. You become more self-aware and most definitely self-conscious. The truth is there is no crash course in attending a historically black college and university

(HBCU). To be honest, I was not ready to deal with the culture. I was in shock. In some cases, I even felt I did not meet the qualifications. These people were from all walks of life, different cities and diverse mentalities. I concluded that it would definitely be a whole new world with a variety of possibilities. It can readily be assumed that this particular environment is not for the weak minded or socially unready.

College, within the HBCU context, is a place that demands the best parts of you to come to the forefront. You are expected to become and to develop your identity. Unfortunately, I would have a lot to learn and to discover about myself. It was apparent. I was 17, tall, black and country. In contrast with people from places like Memphis and other metropolitan areas up north, it was definitely a stark difference between my present environment and me.

The obvious point was that I stuck out like a sore thumb. It was apparent I was the 'nerd' and 'know-it-all.' In class, I was simply deciding to answer questions. After all, we did have engaging classes where I was previously educated. My mother made me take honors and Advanced Placement classes. I simply had the knowledge by default, not because I was trying to be the nerd. I was more concerned with trying to fit in with the culture. After all, that seemed to be the most important place of priority at the time. The majority of my future peers who would become life-long friends hated me, and the fact that I knew what seemed to be "all of the answers", but begged me to help them outside of class. After so many evil glares and snide comments, it began to take a toll on me. No one likes being the social outcast for any reason, especially in college. As African-Americans, we can be so brutal to our own. Day after day, I was teased and picked on all because I decided to read books, instead of play dominoes and smoke blunts. I would study because that was what was expected, instead of skipping class and watching television while treating college like an extended vacation. I was there to accomplish a goal. I was driven to be successful because I chose to go to the college that was actually in direct opposition of my mother. I did not want to hear, "I told you so." Therefore, I refused to give up, so I took the ridicule. It did hurt. The words and the names really hurt. Most people chalk it up to kids just being kids, but that is not the case. I know what it is like to dread walking to class, getting bullied and trying to find alternate ways to get to class without running into certain people. I was 17 and fragile. I was fighting to understand the reason why people who "looked" just like me would treat me as they did. I was not homesick like the normal freshman, I was hurting. Instead of gaining the "Freshmen 15," I lost 15. I was like 110 pounds soaking wet. Looking back, it really did take its toll on me. However, I was actually in basic training regarding how to hold my own. Although painful, it required me to adapt and most importantly position myself accordingly within this new environment that I had chosen for myself. All of a sudden, I realized, like Dorothy on the Wizard of Oz, that I was not in Kansas anymore. My world had shifted and it required a different version of me. I would have to EVOLVE in order to survive.

Life has a way of placing us in new environments with people and predicaments that can be life changing, yet complicated. We are challenged to meet the challenge face-to-face, even amidst, wanting to run and not exactly knowing all that is required of us. We lend ourselves to instinct and tend to go with the flow. However, going with the flow does not always prove the most idealistic strategy. We have to compromise, cooperate and condition ourselves to meet what has been demanded of us. As you approach life day by day, you have to recognize that who you are is subject to change. You will face circumstances that will push you outside of your place of contentment and put you in a place of challenge only to get you to the next level. Places like these places in our lives look huge and life altering. The truth is that every place, in fact, each moment of your life is life altering. You engage change in order to be changed. Change equals process. Process equates progress. Progress extends to evolution to meet the requirement for you to thrive in your future that is readily approaching. Will you feel unready? Yes. Will there be measures of doubt? Yes. Will be people come and go? Yes. Will relationships change? Absolutely.

However, it is all a part of you lending power to your place of change so your life can yield the results of a transformational state of triumph that cannot be denied.

Chapter 2

"Mirror, Mirror....On the Wall"

"What we SEE is not all there IS."
Dr. Robert O'Keefe Hassell

Growing up, I was a very unique child. I was highly inquisitive. I did not take no for an answer. I wanted to know. I was gifted, aware and naturally brilliant. For the first 30 years of my life, I struggled with low self-esteem and my confidence was shot. I knew I did not fit in. I understood that I would never fit in. My perception was distorted because I viewed being "different" as a bad thing when it would actually turn out to what would make me a great person.

'The Ugly Duckling' is one of Danish storyteller Hans Christian Andersen's most famous fairytales. With a powerful message about self-image and acceptance, the story is valued for its ability to teach children the importance of kindness to others. This is the story of a swan born into a family of ducks, who is cast out of the pond because the other animals believe such an "ugly duckling" doesn't belong with them. Wherever he goes, the ugly duckling encounters animals that shun him for the same reason. Upon encountering a group of elegant white birds, the ugly duckling aspires to one day be as beautiful as they are. After a dreadfully cold and lonely winter, the ugly duckling sees his reflection in the water and realizes that he wasn't a duck after all. He has grown to be the most beautiful swan in the pond.

I was the epitome of the 'ugly duckling' or so I perceived. Physically from ages 5-15, I was just oddly shaped. I had skinny legs, a big head, long neck, huge feet and odd features. Not to mention the sheer torment of wearing thick glasses, and when I played sports I wore Horace Grant goggles better known as "Rec-Specs." As a young teen (16-19), I was very self-aware and self-conscious, which I honestly believe was the precursor to me becoming over-analytical and would warp my thinking always trying to reinvent myself as I would head into my adult years. As a young adult in my 20's, I lived my life to prove a point to people and not for my own satisfaction. I wanted to remove all doubt. If you told me I could not do it, I would show you that I could. I was not satisfied with who I "thought" I was at that moment in my life. Nor did I feel that the person I was "becoming" would be good enough for the people whom I cared about and wanted my successes to actually matter. I wanted to feel like I mattered. I wanted to occupy an uncommon space in people's life where both my presence and absence would make a difference. I wanted people to appreciate me on every level. I wanted to be love and wanted to know someone cared.

Looking back in retrospect, I never fit the mold. The struggle was not in changing my perception, but recognizing the definition that being different in so many ways was going to contribute to the outcome of my life. My humanity was in an intensified emotional state because I did not recognize these so called "differences" I felt made me socially unacceptable, yet odd would create avenues of opportunity to reach people in so many unique means in the future. Because my promise and potential was not recognized in its early stages, I like many others, went through trying to piece myself together into what I thought people wanted and would readily accept. Honestly, by doing this, it cost me many years of pain and resentment inwardly. It was a struggle to be socially acceptable. I would have to discover myself piece by piece again after putting down some of the most important parts of myself to pick up something I thought was going to give me the "it factor" as they call it. I would have done better by simply staying true to myself. You live. You learn. You do better. It is just that simple.

The truth is I struggled with validating the person I saw in the mirror. I had difficulty accepting myself. I had problems embracing the truth of who I was in every area of my life. I had problems deciphering between people, personality, position and platform. It was one of the greatest conflicts of my life to date. From my senior year of high school, through my entire college career and even into my early adult life I was seeking for what my life really meant. I wanted that ultimate stamp of approval. I wanted to be recognized, appreciated and know that I counted for something. More so, I really wanted to know if my living made a difference and carried a purpose for being in connection with the people around me that were a part of my life.

Many people will never understand the weight of how a person could be struggling to find meaning for their existence amid so many moving pieces. I would look in the mirror and I would see the oddest shaped individual. Tall, lanky, country, extremely intelligent, and articulate I knew I was a great person. I will be honest with you; I could definitely hide my insecurity well with me being goofy and quite the charmer. I was the epitome of a pro at doing that in a flawless manner! If we can tell the truth, a lot of us mask our insecurities in hopes that somebody will eventually accept the version of ourselves that we have worked so hard to create.

Another group is secure in their own insecurities. This causes them to live their lives in a pitiful state by never escaping to become better, but imprisoning themselves by their own negative perception.

Nevertheless, I fought for years amid sorting through the many questions as to who I really was. Left up to interpretation, it could have been dangerous. In fact, it was dangerous because I did walk on the wild side more than my fair share. I deemed those as calculated periods of recklessness, but it was not ideal and would prove to create delays along the way. Instead of leaving that to chance, I went with what I deemed as a greater risk to take it upon myself to create who I would be. I would be a self-made man. I made up in my mind that the person I would forge myself into would be indisputable, undeniable, unrestricted, respected, even feared and that my name coupled with my presence would speak to the weight of my greatness as a person and professional. For some, that would seem lofty. For others, it would seem ambitious and self-centered. I decided to take the chance of being an over-achiever. I figured it would give me a measure of happiness that I could accept and allow me to accept myself, even amid dealing with my own personal issues regarding self-perception in an unauthentic way. However, for me, that was easily attainable and I had enough fuel to achieve it because of my perception of my environment and willingness to prove a point. Proving a point ended up being a subsequent series of costly processes. It was here I went against both principal and practicality because I wanted people to accept me, but I was presenting a person that was really not me. As a result, I got upset and felt like a failure because no matter what I did, I always seemed to fall short in my own eyes. If you live by the validation and opinions of others, you will surely die by the same. Many times, we place our lives at the feet of the opinions of people not recognizing that they are just opinions, not facts. You only set yourself up to be disappointed and end up in regret when you hinge your life on what people deem to be a necessity when it is not really a priority at all. If you allow it, people will force their opinions to shape your life. If you internalize them, you will become a living experiment. You owe it to yourself to be you! Most importantly, be you for yourself and no one else. You are the one who you need to satisfy. If you are not pleased with yourself, people will have a hard time doing the same.

I honestly believe transparency leads to effective treatment and confession leads to the cure. It is not enough just to see the issue at the surface, but address the reality of what it is we are actually dealing with in our lives. The Story of Snow White and the character of the evil queen can teach us a lot about self-perception and self-realization. When an attempt to satisfy her craving for validation, the evil queen says, "Mirror, Mirror on the wall, who's the fairest of them all?" The mirror is honest and sobering when it reveals that Snow White, and not evil queen, is the fairest. The evil queen then seeks to eradicate Snow White, but only self-destructs in the end.

Our upmost desire is to be wanted and cherished. We want love and security. The social dynamic and hierarchies of our world have caused many of us to place importance on surface rather than substance. We miss cultivating the heart of who we really are because we negate the rawest, authentic self. We have failed to see through the eyes of faith what our heart could become if we actually nurture it through the rough stages. Being that our society is rooted in the superficial, appearance and perception matter the most. We live our lives on a daily basis seeking validation from individuals who are consistently maintaining and portraying an unauthentic image. The core of who we they are is veiled by faulty facades that mask deep inward unresolved struggles. These issues place many of us in a self-consuming cycle because we are readily trying to identify with something that we are not. We are grafting and piecing ourselves together with pieces of identities that are not even ours. We take on personality traits that are detractors and make us appear shallow and out of touch. As a result, people tend not to take us seriously at all. There is always a desperate move made to maintain a visible presence and be seen. We tend to overcompensate trying to prove a point to ourselves that we actually matter and are relevant. The truth is you are relevant only when you make the choice to be who you really are. People appreciate diversity and not duplication. Faking it never worked in anyone's favor. Acknowledging the beauty of your life in every area (i.e. – the good, bad and ugly) will help you appreciate the ever-changing journey of life that is open to endless possibilities through daily working towards progress.

Many of us have a perception problem when it comes to identifying "who we really are" vs. "who we think everybody wants us to be." We wrestle with the reality of ourselves because the hard truth is that we are not all we protract ourselves to be. We become frustrated because it has become too costly to fake it anymore. The pressure that comes with the persona we try to portray is so taxing because the idea of who we are pretending to be is so far-fetched in our own minds. We must understand that we can only be the person we were designed to be nothing more and nothing less. The longer we spend pretending to be someone else, the longer we delay becoming the person we are meant to be.

At some point, just like I did, you will reach a point where you will be forced to ask yourself questions about the current state of your life. It will be uncomfortable, bloody, brutal and extremely confrontational. You must be honest and look at what is true as well as what is not. You cannot live a life of "smoke and mirrors." There is nothing worse than being a fugitive on the run in regards to your own identity. We run from ourselves only to run into the person we were running away from, which was ourselves. I can admit that it is difficult and even scary to face your reality. To grow, you must resign the fact that you must really put it all out there and make up in your mind that you need to change for the better. Embracing the truth of who you are is not something to be afraid of at all. In truth, you will find and know a freedom you have never felt before. If there is anything you cannot deny, it is the face of reality. Once you acknowledge the existence of your own life's reality, you can move forward to places that have been long held up and reach your desired place of growth as an individual.

They say, "Confession is good for the soul." I would say, "When you confess the truth to yourself, you can free the captive that is locked away on the inside." You will reach a point where honesty, in its truest form, will liberate you from current captive places. The truth of the matter is you can never be free until you become honest with where you are. Denial only leads to further detainment. How long will you allow your destiny to be detained because you want to live in the comfort of your own denial? You have to acknowledcge your place of "beginnings" fully, even amid it being your most undesirable place. You cannot deny where you are, or you will never get to where you are going! You can only fool people for so long and you definitely cannot fool yourself. It takes so much energy to live a lie, and the price is too hefty to keep trying to maintain an identity that does not belong to you. Living untruth, fakery of falsehood in regards to self-perception makes it extremely difficult to get to the liberating freedom found in the truth of who you are. You do not have to live a confusing, complicated, frustrating and unsatisfying life. Change your perception. Change your perspective. Change your life.

Chapter 3

"Blurred Lines"

"You don't have to tell yourself the line is CROOKED, especially when you're the one that DREW IT!"

-Dr. Robert O'Keefe Hassell

Geography was always an interesting subject for me. Land masses, mapping, directions, and landforms. History was always engaging for me because of the stories, laws, politics, wars and building of civilizations. History and geography were always interesting because in contrast to my life, they seemingly walked hand in hand. The geography of my life displayed a rough, yet rocky terrain. I was a unique landmass of sorts, yet not fully discovered or cultivated. The beauty of my life had not been seen. The history of my life said I would be great, but the greatness of my life would be shaped my adversity and conflict. I was in control of me. However, the outcome would be determined by who and what I let in. No one ever told me about boundaries and I made the mistake in believing that they would be understood. Soon I discovered that having those necessary boundaries would prevent total takeover from people with ulterior motives, forcefully entering into negative relationships, and ultimately consumed by cycles that would lead to devastating destruction.

I was 19 when I pledged a Black-Greek Letter Organization (BGLO). I am a proud member of Phi Beta Sigma Fraternity, Inc. It was indeed a social rite of passage. It brought about many changes. I went from being known in an average sense into the direct spotlight with a set of new social standards to uphold.

However, my letters were not a definition of me, but brought out the fullness of my identity though enhancing what was already there. Needless to say, it brought about its fair share of experiences both good and bad. I will be honest; it brought out the wild, risky and reckless side of me. It was an 'evolutionary change' that would occur to push me to the brink of subsequent changes I would make as an adult man. I would learn so many lessons that would follow me forever. In college and my early 20's, people were somewhat like revolving doors. In between pledging a BGLO, being intensely involved in campus-student life and popular, puts quite a spin on your little life. After all, I had come a long way since freshman year. It was total life shift with a new attitude. In my case, I was very analytical and observant. Nevertheless, I used my charm to be quite diplomatic and I was one heck of a negotiator. I simply used what I had to get what I wanted. It was not the most ideal philosophy to live by, but for a college graduate abruptly thrust into the mainstream of society it seemed to work in my favor. Translating into life after college, which could be a recipe for disaster. You have the tendency to end up connected to people under the wrong pretense and thereby end up in some unhealthy cycles.

After graduating, I came into adulthood off the wind of popularity and a fresh college grad. I had a job coming right out of school because of seizing an opportunity from successfully completing two internship terms. I was literally on cloud nine. After acceptance into graduate school, boundaries were totally out of the picture. I thought I was in control; however, I was out of control. The lack of those strong relationships, mentors and confidantes in my life would follow me into my mid and late 20's. It had become the norm for people to come and go. I had it together on the surface, but personally this would be another change that would lead to the next phase of my EVOLUTION.

From 2007 to 2010, I was on a roller coaster ride. I refer to this time as my roaring 20's. I remember ages 21, 24, and 25. In retrospect, the years I do remember just blend together in what I call the blur. In my own mind, I ruled the world and everything was at my fingertips. To an outsider looking at me, it would most definitely seem that way. However, looking at it in reality, I was stretched and had no boundaries. I could be who I wanted and I would go out of my way to prove to the furthest extent of who I was (not to mention what I could do).

I found myself over-compensating because I was losing ground.

Boundaries are always necessary! The truth is the commonality leads to areas of compromise on every level. It is okay to be optimistic, but it is troublesome to be in a state of reckless euphoria hoping that everything will work like in a fairy tale. Life has a way of making the 'fairy tale' become just that, a fairy tale. It is nice to think about, pleasant to consider, but it is not your reality. When you learn to not only live, but also deal in reality, you will find that you can truly experience where you are, what you are, and what you need to be. When we lack boundaries, we are not only vulnerable, but also susceptible to situations that cause us to lose control of the most vital parts of our lives.

EVOLVE

Currently, we believe if there are no boundaries the greater the possibility to acquire more. Our appetites for people, possessions and positions can be so insatiable. We are willing to sacrifice the most meaningful parts of ourselves to obtain an illusion of grandeur, which turns out to be entirely less than we expected. Additionally, we find ourselves indebted to an underlying system and sometimes bound to a thing that we never expected to join to at all. Nothing can bring people together like crisis, confusion and chaos. These things are the temporary bonds that fasten issues to us and can delay our progress all because we have failed to draw the lines in the sand.

Boundaries equate a measure of consistency that allows us to be in a place of continual self-control. Self-control is necessary for our success, and safety on every level. Yes, I took risk and suffered the consequences. Failed relationships, bad judgement calls, and mistakes are where you take a tremendous hit. We wager and risk ourselves by aligning ourselves to others for the sake of security, stability and the hope of sanity. We create a life premised on co-dependency. We become too grafted into other people and places that we get to the point where we cannot possibly imagine life without them. Our mere existence is tied into them. There is no divide, distinction or definition. Consequently, this is a course to a path of self-destruction. The lack of self-control brings about adversaries that threaten our peace of mind, and our future. We as human beings are thinkers by nature and we have the ability to reason. Although our ability to reason with clarity is sometimes by our free will, we tend to make decisions that are less than rational. In fact, they are irrational and even borderline insane. If we do not take measures to determine that we will not act out of impulse, we place ourselves in a state of conundrum. We lose our ability to feel, and there is no consideration for others around us. Additionally, there is no level of remorse concerning our decisions and subsequent actions that may affect multiple parties.

We must understand we live in a world that requires operating in certain roles so we can feasibly co-exist with each other without drastic levels of interference. Yes, there will be interference and levels of conflict because of differences in personality and preference. However, these boundaries keep us from committing acts and succumbing to places of temptation that look good to us, but are not good for us. Think of how many times we ended up in unexpected places because we were negligent and decided to neglect the safety of having boundaries. Many of us would have saved time, energy, money and lots of stress had we not yielded ourselves to these places of influence.

As a young man, in my early 20's, I felt invincible. I was reckless, carefree and did not consider many consequences of my actions. Honestly, I did everything I was big and bad enough to do. I was a rebel. I was radical. I was rational. Truthfully, by me being rational, it allowed me to refocus and rebound through what I really consider one of the most tumultuous times of my life. When you are young, you do not think and you believe you have all the time in the world. You believe that if something does not go well, you can immediately exchange or replace them.

Looking back, half of the stuff I did was simply because I could do it and get away with it. The thrill of it all was simply icing on the cake. I found myself extending myself to people in exchange for love, appreciation, and validation. I was always placing myself in a place of "proving" and going to the furthest extent to eliminate any doubt as to who I was. I wanted to have something to call my own. I wanted to have power. Being so young and self-consumed, I lived by the phrase, "Use what you have, to get what you want." In retrospect, that was an extremely compromising position to place myself in on so many levels. My life had started to become a revolving door. I was emotionally hanging on to small pieces of myself by threads and trying to reason over the fact, I had given up so much because I had consented to allow people to take from me.

It is through boundaries that we are able to develop a consistent measure of accountability and discipline, which will greatly benefit us as we pursue our future goals. We can only accomplish those goals when we learn how to co-exist within the dynamics of our society. Each day we encounter a variety of social structures lending ourselves to determine which roles we will play, how far we will go, and the calculated risk and decisions we will make to achieve and maintain a desired goal. Not having the proper boundaries in your life will put you in a place to be overtaken by life, and by opportunist people. You have to learn how to regulate your actions and interactions towards others. Boundaries will enable you to practice an active measure of discipline by keeping you from giving into indulgences and desires on a whim. It will keep you and your life together. We must never negate that self-control is an important aspect of self-development. Although self-control is ongoing, it is the key to further development. As you reinforce the necessary boundaries in your life, the more self-control and discipline will be demonstrated.

Too many of us allow people to deplete us because we fail to constantly assess the nature of the relationship and establish the appropriate boundaries. We consent and give access to people who should not have it. We consent to support people who will only use our influence to attract more attention to them. Little do you know that while you are consistently giving, there is nothing being given back to you. Then you wake up one day feeling empty handed, by yourself, felling manipulated and even confused.

Additionally, we tend to fall into places of emotional inconsistency that lead to places of depression, isolation, bitterness and resentment. We put ourselves in a place of self-torment and intense turmoil when our emotions consume our being by driving us to a place of hopelessness. In reality, we must make decisions that are clearly 'black and white' without compromise. Yes, most of the decisions we make are tough because we have established faulty, yet fragmented connections we infused in our lives that feel good and they do not fit! By living life in this "clouded" state, we can become jaded to the fact of our present reality.

EVOLVE

If we want to see growth, we must accept the responsibility of securing and establishing boundaries. It's okay to say, "No." In life, no matter what we do, if we are truly sincere there is a risk of becoming overzealous even for a positive cause. There comes a time when you must evaluate the integrity of your relationships with people. If you are not in a relationship or friendship where reciprocity abides continually, you are wasting your time and you're headed to a place called depletion.

Blurred lines are dangerous because there is no distinction between the person, the purpose, the plan and the final product. Boundaries speak to the definitive places in our life. They determine what we will and will not accept. They determine the lines we will not cross in friendships and relationships. They are our standards that are manifested. We yield ourselves to trouble and disappointment when we make concessions in places where there should be no compromise because there are boundaries in place.

It is important that we always tell ourselves the truth regarding the fragile boundaries we have established, no matter how much it hurts. The reason we hesitate in telling ourselves the truth is because it is a confrontational occurrence. A period of re-adjustment may require the end of specific relationships we invested in over time. The truth is confrontational and unavoidable, but it can provide the way out of the cycle that is readily consuming us. It is a necessary meeting with the reality of who we are, what is in our space, what is influencing us, who actually has control and our current state in life. The truth is constantly being revealed and being unfolded in our lives whether we choose to accept it or not. To

EVOLVE

except truth is to grow, but to deny it is to remain

stagnant and eventually die.

Chapter 4

"The Enemy INNER Me!"

"I FOUGHT. I WON. I LIVED to TELL about it!"

Dr. Robert O'Keefe Hassell

Our insecurities can be our greatest enemies. We live in a self-centered and selfish generation. We are obsessed with looks and superficial things that do not amount to much of anything. Social media allows us to paint the picture of perfection amid our inconsistency, real-life-problems and inability to communicate. We hide behind filters and the appearance of happiness, but are struggling to find self-satisfaction, fulfillment and hope that one day our lives will really become what we portray them to be. We have become inflated, narcissistic and unable to perceive the world outside of ourselves. If we are not careful, we can become shallow and stagnant. Contrary to popular belief, people can always see the truth beyond what you seek to hide through overcompensating.

Realistically, most of us struggle with the fact that we are inadequate in some way and or are rough on the edges. We badger ourselves daily and always press ourselves regarding that one shortcoming and daily negate the progress we are making. Whether you recognize it or not, your life is becoming something different each day. A new part of you is unfolding and greatness is breaking through in ways you cannot even imagine. However, in order to be triumphant in our daily walk and our journey through this life, we must be able to confront and conqueror these places of insecurity. If we fail to this, it will readily consume us without fail. Many times, we become our own worst enemy when we seek to compare and contrast our lives to others. Each one of us has a pace. No matter how much we desire to be like another individual, we cannot. Each of our lives carries us to places of commonality, but we have a unique distinction that will help us leave a mark on the world we live in every day.

We live in a world that seeks to define you before you even have the chance to discover who you really are. If you are not careful, that can be ammunition to literally assassinate your potential and promise before you have a chance to thrive. The most prevalent area that caught my attention was my last name. My last name is Hassell. It is not an appealing name; nevertheless, it is associated with being troublesome and tedious even though the spelling is different. What I did know is that there was a stigma behind my last name. Growing up, people never said it to our faces, but the looks were enough at times. They knew whose son I was and who my father was. Being a single male child in the family, and living under a stigma can cause you to take unconventional paths to prove otherwise. I knew that opinion and scrutiny would be thrust upon me. I knew there would be people who would plot and position themselves to ensure I would end up in the same cycle as my father. Others were simply waiting and watching every move wondering how my mother would succeed in raising a man without a male-factor in the home. Honestly speaking, there were more spectators than supporters. My childhood was plagued with many traumas ranging from drugs to domestic violence. Moreover, addiction through its full weight was an attempt to destroy any possibility of who my two sisters and I would become. However, it did not win. We prevailed. My mother was very consistent in her way of sustaining consistency in chaotic environments. She was a consistent fixture reminding us continually, that no matter how our life would fall, we always had a scaffold in place to rebuild. To this day, this is why I believe people look at me and the word struggle never crosses their mind.

Despite how we turned out, and my mother's efforts to shield us, there were places I had to face. Those places tested me as a man in every area of my existence. Honestly, I fought every single day of my life from ages 17-31 to defeat the entity I had magnified against my future, which was my own self coupled with my insecurities. Insecurity can be the fortress that holds our greatest adversary. If we are not careful, these immeasurable amounts of insecurity will gain an advantage and eventually consume us by convincing us of who we are not. As a result, we will live under the oppression of a continual identity crisis until we make up in our minds to fight back.

From my teens, I had internalized specific places of insecurity that would follow me into my adult life. The constant pursuit of these made my life behind closed doors a real battlefield. I had learned how to wear a public face very well, but I had difficulty dealing and processing through private pain. Truthfully, I never felt good enough. I did not feel valued. The majority of the time I felt invisible even being around people. People could never tell because I was the "life and the light" in the room. I overcompensated in my goofiness coupled with charm. No matter how much joy I had in those moments, I had to face the reality of my own places of despair behind the scenes. I would spend the next 14 years of my life making the attempts to prove myself to myself. Proving myself to others in the process would simply be icing on the cake. In making the attempt to prove a point, in turn, it would take the joy out of some of my life's greatest accomplishments and milestones.

Honestly, all I have accomplished thus far is that I was reaching to find meaning for my life. I defined myself by the measure of success I could potentially achieve, while trying to convince myself I was actually worth something. I let my pain fuel my ambition. I had "daddy issues." I felt less than a man at times. I still felt like that odd, quirky adolescent who was unprepared to stand. Affirmation and validation proved to be a place of pain for me. I longed to hear those words, "I'm proud of you son!" I wish I could hear, "O'Keefe, son I love you." Most people would excuse it by saying, "A father's love is just understood." However, that seemed to evade me. It was one of those things that were seemingly taken in stride even though I knew there was more. I could not trace the love because it was never expressed. It was a phenomenon, maybe even a theory. Nevertheless, it was a love that I could not feel. The truth is I did have a biological dad, but I did not have a father. Reflecting back, that is the reason I struggled so much in my personal life. Just like in The Theory of Evolutionary, it was a place of a "bad mutation." If the change is harmful during a bad mutation, then it is unlikely that the offspring will survive to reproduce, so the mutation dies out and goes nowhere. Just like that, life in my 20's, despite how much I was achieving in the public eye, hit a dead halt. Honestly, I became numb and lacked the ability to feel. I woke up day after day knowing that I existed, but could not sense the present moment and fully embrace it beyond just existing. Due to my relationship with my father and our home life growing up, I began to become angry and resentful. It plagued me for years, despite the smile on my face in public. It was no secret that my father struggled with issues surrounding drugs, domestic violence and illegal activity. As a result, it placed us in some crazy places and even put our lives at risk many times. The anger I held pushed me to overcompensate and become bitter in the process. I vowed never to be like the man who gave life to me in any shape, form or fashion. However, as my body changed, he was the reflection I saw in the mirror. Each day, I longed for my reflection to change. The reality is that he was a part of me, but he was not me. Recognizing who I was beyond what happened to me, was the battle that would rage inside of me for years until I reached 31.

Honestly, I needed my dad to be my dad. The one I could confide in and ask what being a man was about. No one could teach me the lessons that he could. I believe if we would have been close and had a relationship, I would not have faced some issues or dealt with situations that I could have altogether avoided. Looking back, my resilience to even open my eyes to face another day during this time was amazing to me. There was divine protection from many things in my life. Hence the saying, "God protects babes and fools." I was definitely both, no doubt. However, some vivid realities and people were constant reminders of what my father was. They took every opportunity to do it. It was hurtful and painful to endure on a regular basis. Through every laugh and subliminal put down, it was like continual kicks and punches. Stronger than I thought, I was able to bear the wounding because of turning my pain into power. I was determined to prove them wrong and prove myself right in my own eyes. I had to fight for who I would become. Plainly stated, I had to show them better than I could tell them! Although it seemed as if I was outnumbered in perception and public opinion, my mantra was the following: "Watch me prove you wrong!" It was an unshakeable, yet a focused resolve. It made me relentless, intense and pushed me to maintain a steady proactive plan with multiple options. Just like the Theory of Evolution says, "If the change is beneficial, then it is likely that the offspring will do better than other offspring and so will reproduce more. Through reproduction, the beneficial mutation spreads. The process of culling bad mutations and spreading good mutations is called natural selection" (Wood, 2002). It was a beneficial, yet painful resolve to not only be better, but do better. My goal was to remove all doubt. In the end, I was successful but it came at a price. The greatest pieces of me as a person would drastically shift to push me into my next place. It was a catalyst once again for me to EVOLVE.

Chapter 5

"Life Beyond the Dirt: GROW through It!"

"Your DIRT was never the DECIDING FACTOR concerning your DESTINY!"

Dr. Robert O'Keefe Hassell

Dirt is a mixture of a whole lot of "stuff" such as rocks, sand, clay, and organic matter. The characteristics of the dirt depend on the weather, the combinations of rocks, sands and clays, your geographic location, and what kind of organic matters are in the soil. It is the climate that has a major effect on the breakdown of solid materials. Dirt is actually a seed's most valuable resource even amid its undesirable qualities. Each of us is dealt a hand in life. We enter into this world with promise. These are seeds. How it develops in our formative years is cultivated through our experiences. A seed is

63

an embryonic plant enclosed in a protective outer covering. The formation of the seed is part of the process of reproduction in seed plants. A seed is a flowering plant's unit of reproduction, capable of developing into another such plant. I have come to realize that 'dirt' is a place of definition. Dirt is a place of destiny.

Dirt is a place of difficulty. One of the most difficult things about being a human is that we live in a world where weaknesses are deemed permanent. We are groomed and engineered to show no signs of vulnerability. The understanding has been generated that any sign of weaknesses deems us both inefficient and ineffective. Our weaknesses make us feel powerless and in some cases hopeless. You cannot deny your dirt. It is a part of who you are and is the place that feeds your growth. Life's dirt is a defining moment for each of us. Either we can gather the beneficial lessons that come from it, or allow our dreams to die under the pretense of accepting our shortcomings as permanent. It is the dirt of our lives that give way to the development of our character, test our approach and attitude amid difficult situations, and cause us to see as well as live beyond what we feel.

If we were transparent, we caused some situations resulting in a setback or delay. We have made mistakes, some worse than others. We have had those lapses in judgement and took risk. In all actuality, they cost some of us more than expected and it came with a high price. There are events in our lives that were also set in motion through the adversity of our decisions that were not within the realm of our control. These are what I called the "after-shocks" of life. These require us, as seedlings, to push through to break the surface. It is only after we have broken the surface that we can become and bloom beautifully into what we were destined to become.

My mid-20's to 31 were a time of self-discovery, self-doubt, constant re-adjustment, seeking validation, over-thinking and definitely a place of irrational decision making surrounded by a central goal of eventually trying to become somebody in the future. Honestly, my ultimate goal was to make the family name untarnished. As the only boy amid my dad's decisions, I felt it was my responsibility as a man to overcome the perceptions of people to prove a point, so neither my family nor I would not be "labeled" as a mistake. It made me ambitious. Honestly, I struggled so much trying to craft and identity as a man in the "rocky ground" of an example that my father left me. It was really hard. No blue prints. No guides. No tips. I had to define my personal meaning of manhood in contrast with the realities life presented me. It was filled with many twist and turns. I readily expected it, but I was still scared and even naïve. However, it forced me to become resourceful, aware, appreciative and keen. My mental prowess sharpened because I was required to think as my decisions and actions carried the weight of accountability and were a direct reflection of what was being invested. My motivation was to be not only a man by definition, but a man in its truest sense.

It took a lot of work. I struggled to fashion and forge myself to be acceptable first and then seek validation. Looking back, I was accepted more than

I thought. I was odd and quite different in so many ways. However, people loved these things the most about me. I saw things differently. I never saw problems in people, but I saw opportunities and the ability to become better. My optimism was through the roof. I could see progress. But I failed to see the same in myself because I lacked validation and affirmation in some of the most necessary places of my life. Validation, if you do not have it within yourself, can become a place of severe vulnerability. It can place you in a weak place and at the mercy of who you submit yourself to. It can lead to people labeling you and you living under the label for extended periods of time. Sometimes we can become so adamant on seeking validation from others that we forget to appreciate the real beauty of the person we really are. We discount it because we do not look, sound or appear like the rest. The truth is you were not created to be a clone. Everyone is not the same. You gain a greater appreciation for yourself when you take the time to recognize and nurture who you are. Appreciate the growth opportunities in the place you are in and do not curse your place of current difficulty or disappointment. Push! Fight! Extend yourself the opportunity to grow. You have to will yourself beyond what you see. Everything you see is not all that there is. Do not be so easily deceived by your senses or surroundings. Appreciate each place and what it has to show you not only about where you are headed, but about yourself.

You have to appreciate the person that you are! Never discount you value or place in life. You matter to more people than you think. There were several times in my life that I doubted that on so many occasions. However, as I boldly continued to discover who I really was, I understood the value in knowing self-worth and its direct connection to reaching the place of fulfillment within your life. We have to learn to live beyond people's expectations and opinions of us. Do not let the expectations of others pressure you into positions and places that you are not ready for at all. Do not let their opinions cause you to make rash decisions to abate what they might say or pacify their perceptions regarding the course of your life. It is your life! You have to live with the decisions you make. Unfortunately, their opinions are not going to confront the reality that you are going to have to face. Your life is moving forward. You may be in the same place, but time and opportunity are always in motion. You cannot afford to sit by idly and expect change or progress in your life. You play an active role in the pursuit of your change. Give yourself the space to grow. Pursue your dreams without fail and do not let anyone pull you away from your place of fulfillment. You owe it to yourself to live.

Some people say, "O'Keefe, you make it look really easy?" Has life been easy? No. It is quite difficult. Living takes a lot work. Have I cried? Yes, so many tears I could literally drown in them. Did I want to give up? Absolutely, more times than I can actually count. Have I second-guessed myself? Yes, even after reaching a place of clarity. Has the journey been worth it? Without a doubt, it truly has. We never know the depth and scope of our abilities until life puts us to the test. Unfortunately, there is no prep class for life's test. There is no official grading system. It is either pass or fail. If you fail, you simply re-take it. I have learned so much in my 31 years, but I recognize there is still much more to learn. Life is one big lesson. Truthfully, you LEARN as you LIVE and LIVE as you LEARN! This is what makes LIFE worth LIVING! Recognizing this, you will EVOLVE!

Chapter 6

Metamorphosis: "CHANGE That Happens In A Place Called NOW!"

"How does one become a butterfly? They have to want to learn to fly so much that you are willing to give up being a caterpillar."

Unknown

Someone asked me, "O'Keefe, how does it feel to be where you are now? What lessons did you learn? What does it take to be you?" Actually, I was sort of at a loss for words. Nevertheless, there is a first time for everything. Normally, I am a pro at layered questions, but this answer proved to be quite difficult for me. This was a question that made me question every layer and dimension of my human existence. It really made me focus on the simplicity of my life and examine who I am.

Contrary to popular belief or what some people interpret by their perceptions, I am an actual human being. I have feelings. I am human. I bleed. I make mistakes. I get back up. Honestly, there is never a moment that I am not learning. I am discovering who I am, not through the eyes of others, but through my own eyes. I am seeing some of the most unique parts of who I am at the core of my being develop each day. Additionally, I am seeing the nature of my flaws as well as opportunities for growth.

Becoming who I am in the present, came about with a tremendous amount of sacrifice and so much pain. There were more days that I actually second guessed my life plan and who I really was while making strides to achieve it. In public, I was courageous. I wore my abilities well. However, behind closed doors, I was fragile and life was so "weighty" that it could not even be put into words. It was an indescribable pain and with so many feelings attached. I felt alone and misunderstood. I did not have anyone to talk to or at least it felt that way. I did not want to be judged, stereotyped or categorized because I had questions or admitted places of my own personal weakness. After all, I did not have the space to be weak. Honestly, there was no viable place of refuge in sight. I had to grow up quick and develop a plan. Not only to be a man, but become the man that my mother, grandmother and 2 sisters would need. It was a lot to think about at times. I rarely could focus on myself, so I chose who I would need to be. The more things happened in my life, the more my choices were strategically made and initiated.

I not only had to be a man, but I had to prove it. I could have chosen to be the rebel. I could have decided to "thug it out," have a couple of baby mama's and kids, get involved in drugs, stay in the streets and stay in trouble. However, I knew there was something greater and most of all better that awaited me. I did not have to "live out" what seemed to be the most popular accepted way or proving your manhood without a shadow of a doubt. The path I chose was undeniable success. I chose ambition. I chose Church. I chose God. It was hard for me because I did not look like the rest or sound like them. I definitely did not have the "Barry White" (voice). I was always the "Best-friend." I was the wise counsel and sensible person. I was the soundboard for everyone's life-altering decisions. I was not the dominant, yet over-bearing type. I was the nerd. The church-boy. I had a big heart. In most instances, I was viewed as passive because I did not choose aggression, but I chose self-control and peaceable solutions. I had seen authority abused and used as control. I refused to be that way because of certain examples that came before me in childhood. I swore never to be that kind of man. I went to the furthest extent to not be that kind of man because I had 2 little sisters and I was the one permanent fixture of a man that they saw on a regular basis. I refuse to be compared or contrasted with anything I had seen before. I was determined to forge my own identity as a man while proving a point at the same time. Was I successful? Yes. Did it cost me? Yes, more than you will ever know.

As an adolescent, young adult and eventually an adult man it was really hard to hear or legitimately

receive the phrases: "O'Keefe, you did so well!";
"O'Keefe, I love you and I mean it!" (outside of my immediate family); "O'Keefe, I care."; "O'Keefe, I value your place in my life."; O'Keefe, I appreciate what you did and who you are!"; "O'Keefe, you have so much in you and I want the best for you."; "Dr. Hassell, you performed and executed with such skill today."; Dr. Hassell, I cannot wait for you to work with me on this project; "Hassell".....followed by some form of flattery that I would roll my eyes at on the regular.

It was hard discerning motives of people, developing trust and extending myself. The irony is that I could always see the best in other people, but I never could see it in myself. It was the most frustrating thing at times. I would give and continuously give. I believe that if you sowed good, even amid the bad, the good will sprout up one day when they need it the most. People would always say, "Why would you do that for them? Why go there when they do not even like you? They are using you and you don't even see it! You are doing too much and need to slow down?" All the while, I would smile and be like, "Me? Stop? For what?" I would even help my known enemies, especially the people that would praise you when you saved them but talk about you afterwards. I always lived by the principle of "doing right" by people and not for the sake of being the sainted hero, but because I believed in genuinely being good. I simply wanted to be what I desperately needed, but did not have when I was at the many different phases in my life. There never were any agendas or ulterior motives to gain anything from anybody.

I now know that I could not process it because I could not feel or reconcile it past my own perspectives. Being a man, at its foundation, meant protecting myself. Most importantly, protecting myself and my interest at all cost. Therefore, I intentionally blocked people. I had built up impenetrable walls and compartmentalized my life to afford people accessible places that I could control. The reason why this happened is because during critical stages of my life, people that were assigned to carry me in some form or fashion dropped me. In most of those cases, I was able to recover and do it quick. My determination played a critical role in that resilience. Nevertheless, I had internal injuries that would have to be healed so I could be whole again. The walls were a measure of safety for me and it did not allow me to be hurt, manipulated or abused. It was a defense mechanism, which was totally non-aggressive. However, it could be viewed as nonchalant, disengaged and disconnected to outsiders.

I was Super-Man and Clark Kent in the same day! Some people attached to Super-Man, so they never saw Clark Kent. Few people saw Clark Kent ever and those that did barely understood the depth of my humanity in its fullness. I wish I could tell people it was easy, but then I would be telling one of the biggest lies ever. There is so much that has happened to me and around me it actually amazes me at times that I am still standing. There were many things that happened to me along the way that are even beyond my ability to put into words. I can say though, "I did not die, I have lived to come out on the other side of it and I am learning to embrace what life is really intended to be." The process was rigorous. The defeats were devastating. I know all too well what it is like to have everything collapse into a pile of rubble and be required to appear as if everything is fine. I know what it is like to be torn apart from the inside out, yet have to fix your face like a flint and do what is required of you. It was during these times that I actually discovered that I was way stronger than I thought. I lost friendships, ones that I treasured and even grieve over until this day. In time, I have made peace with it though and I believe that everything will come around for the good again. I have had to reconcile destiny and decision on so many occasions it makes my head swim even thinking about it again.

The most valuable part of my evolutionary process was my mistakes. Man, I have made so many

EVOLVE

I have lost count. Pride. Naïve. Broken relationships. Misguided motives. Bitterness coupled with resentment. Giving up. Being quick-tempered and slick-mouthed (at times). Too smart for my own good. Contrary to what some might say, I believe that mistakes are necessary. My mistakes have prompted me to step up to the learning curve quick. Mistakes tend to uproot or upset the apparent idea of invincibility that we have developed for ourselves. It is an immediate snap-back to reality. It is at this place where you become willing and open to new perspectives that you previously failed to see. Furthermore, it assists us in internalizing the truth without resistance. It is only after we make the mistake that we are willing to learn or try it a different way. Depending on what happens as a result of our mistake we are utterly convinced to avoid the level of pain associated with the mistake at all cost. Mistakes will teach you while molding you at the same time. The truth is that mistakes are unavoidable and there will be occasions where you make them albeit intentionally or unintentionally. Nevertheless, they serve the same purpose which is to teach you. Sometimes the collateral damage from them can be devastating. However, I would consider it sort of like the "demolition phase" when you make strides to complete a home improvement or upgrade. Sometimes you fail to see the real issue at hand or how things could in fact be better until you make the mistake. Mistakes will definitely break and fracture you in some places. I definitely know mine have on many occasions. Mistakes hurt and some of them hurt really bad. It's not necessarily outward hurt, but the inward hurt that takes a while to heal. Those "heart" kind of hurts and mental traumas. It is not so easy to forget or get past. However, time gives you the space to gain the necessary strength back.

We also have to recognize that some things are not our fault. Too many times we penalize ourselves because of the things that have happened to us. We live our lives swirled around "What if's? "Why me's? "Why Now's? And "Will I ever?" We continually run these questions and cripple the progress of our own lives because we fail to step out and become the answer that we need. Nevertheless, life is made beautiful by you picking up the pieces and creating something beautiful out of it. The reality is that everybody will not be the same and that is okay. God defines your purpose and orders your steps. You are responsible for giving your life meaning. Now that I am here, I am finding myself reflecting back on the journey and trying to re-discover the values of those moments by interpreting what they mean to my ever-evolving present. One thing I did come to understand is that life does not stop at any milestone achievement or at one single point of overcoming. However, when the moment has passed and the sun rises the next day, that is your signal that the clock is still ticking and there is still another victory to be obtained.

IMPORTANT

this week

this month

someday

REFERENCES

Bogin, B. 1999. Evolutionary perspective on human growth. Ann. Rev. Anthropol. 28:109-153.

Wood, W., & Eagly, A. H. (2002). A cross-cultural analysis of the behavior of women and men: Implications for the origin of sex differences. *Psychological Bulletin*, 128, 699-727.

Made in the USA
Columbia, SC
28 October 2018